Write Away

From Hurt to Heel'd

Guided Journal for emotional Health Happiness & Healing

The Write away guided Journal is a collaboration with Just Keep Writing Publishing & B Heel'd Productions

Just Keep Writing
Publishing

Write Away

B HEEL'D

Overwhelmed with the weight of my emotions I cried uncontrollably as I removed my shoe and threw it across the room. In this moment my sole desire was to express how angry I was because I made a bad decision. During the height of my tantrum I experienced the calming peace of God as he spoke to me saying "give it to me". I instantly began to evaluate my behavior and ask myself why I was so mad at the shoe as if it made the bad decision. With a calm heart I stood to collect the shoe and put it away as God spoke to me again. He told me to give him all of my hurt and pain so he could heal me. I walked into the closet carefully looking down at all of the shoes. Standing still evaluating the space God spoke telling me to look around, as I obeyed I become aware of the variation of shoes. So much purpose packed in one place I intentionally examined the high heels, low heels, flats and sneakers, unmoving in my moment it hit me…B Heel'd. God wanted to reach me in a way that I could comprehend. I suddenly understood that like all the different types of shoes there are different levels and steps to the healing process. God loves me so much that he wanted to go in and repair me from all the different situations that hurt me. I spell it different because we all heal differently. My steps may not be yours and yours may not be mine. But, we all experience hurt and if we do not work towards healing from the things that hurt us we will injure ourselves and others along the way. Until this moment I did not fully understand something my pastor said about 9 years ago "Childhood hurt becomes grown up pain". I realized that I am responsible for me just as you are for yourself and we can choose healing at anytime. The process may be uncomfortable but it is worth it I challenge you to join me on the journey. Live Heel'd and victory shall always be yours.

-Belarria Eichelberger

Caterpillar

Decide that you want it more than you are afraid of it.
- Bill Cosby

From Hurt to Heel'd

Nothing just happens! There is no magic pill that heals our emotions. We are always responsible for our spiritual, mental and emotional health. Think of the guided journal as an emotional cleanse, there will be discomfort but it is worth it. As you start the process remember to be patient with yourself and do not rush the process. There is no time restraint to your healing, no one is judging you. We challenge you to Connect with your faith and dig deep into your heart to release the bad while affirming the good. Each journal section is divided into four areas defined below. Complete the journals and activities in any order while keeping your goals in mind. No matter how tough it may seem at times you have within you everything you need to move from hurt to healed.

Reflect

Self reflection is vital in the healing journey. Each section of the write away journal begins with the difficult task of facing self. The goal of the reflection section is to set the tone for areas of improvement while working towards total healing.

Release

Most often we pack down the emotional wounds instead of releasing them. Releasing does not mean that it may not still hurt sometimes, it simply frees the space for healing to enter. This section is most useful after a long day or emotional upset. You have the power at any time to let it go!

Affirm

Affirmations set the atmosphere for gratitude. Sometimes it's difficult to speak good things about yourself. The affirm section challenges you to speak only good using " I AM" declarations. Use this section to start your day with positive self reflection.

Connect

One of the main barriers to healing is isolation. Connecting with your faith is vital in the healing journey. In the connect sections you are encouraged to nurture intentional communication with God. Nothing about you surprises God, allow yourself to connect with him in a deeper way.

Plan, Focus, Grow

Designate a specific day and time for writing, be realistic but also challenge yourself. Successful journaling is all about consistently committing to your process. Use the table below to outline your writing schedule for one week.

Day	Time	Focus *Circle only one per day*
Monday Date :___/___/____	_____:_____AM _____:_____PM	Reflect Affirm Release Connect
Tuesday Date :___/___/____	_____:_____AM _____:_____PM	Reflect Affirm Release Connect
Wednesday Date :___/___/____	_____:_____AM _____:_____PM	Reflect Affirm Release Connect
Thursday Date :___/___/____	_____:_____AM _____:_____PM	Reflect Affirm Release Connect
Friday Date :___/___/____	_____:_____AM _____:_____PM	Reflect Affirm Release Connect
Saturday Date :___/___/____	_____:_____AM _____:_____PM	Reflect Affirm Release Connect
Sunday Date :___/___/____	_____:_____AM _____:_____PM	Reflect Affirm Release Connect

Identify one action, feeling or thought you would like to work on this week. Use the section below to outline your area of growth and remember to review it at the end of the week.

Grow

This week I will work on positive: **Feelings   Actions   Thoughts**

What is one thing I can do this week to achieve positive progress?

_____

_____

_____

Reflect
Who am I?

_____
_____
_____
_____
_____
_____
_____
_____
_____
_____
_____
_____
_____
_____
_____
_____
_____
_____
_____
_____
_____
_____
_____
_____
_____
_____

*Use this space to declare good things, write where you wish to be &
encourage yourself as if you are already there.*

Check Point

Focus
(*Select one focus word*)

☐ *Faith*   ☐ *Trust*

☐ *Freedom* ☐ *Patience*

Define your focus:
(*briefly describe what your focus word means to you*)

_____

_____

_____

_____

3 Ways I will focus on _____ today?

1. _____

2. _____

3. _____

Why is this focus important to me?
_____
_____
_____
_____
_____
_____

Self Care Challenge
Take 10 minutes today and focus only on your focus word. Create a peaceful place for the good to grow. Allow yourself to run wild with the desire to achieve your focus goal today!

Release

Psalm 107:28-30
Then they cried out to the lord in their trouble, and he brought them out of their distress. He stilled the storm to a whisper; the waves of the sea were hushed. They were glad when it grew calm, and he guided them to their desired haven.

What are you struggling with today? What difficult emotions have you battled this week?

_____

_____

_____

_____

_____

_____

_____

_____

_____

_____

_____

_____

_____

_____

_____

_____

_____

_____

_____

_____

_____

_____

_____

Connect

Prayer is the best connection to God. -Author Unknown

Dear God,

_____

_____

_____

_____

_____

_____

_____

_____

_____

_____

_____

_____

_____

_____

_____

_____

_____

_____

_____

_____

_____

_____

_____

_____

_____

Mirror, Mirror

I am a Mirror for Love and Light,
but never for Anger or Fear.
- Jonathan Lockwood Huie

Plan, Focus, Grow

Designate a specific day and time for writing, be realistic but also challenge yourself.
Successful journaling is all about consistently committing to your process. Use the table below to
outline your writing schedule for one week.

Day	Time	Focus *Circle only one per day*	
Monday Date :___/___/____	_____:_____AM _____:_____PM	Reflect Affirm Release Connect	
Tuesday Date :___/___/____	_____:_____AM _____:_____PM	Reflect Affirm Release Connect	
Wednesday Date :___/___/____	_____:_____AM _____:_____PM	Reflect Affirm Release Connect	
Thursday Date :___/___/____	_____:_____AM _____:_____PM	Reflect Affirm Release Connect	
Friday Date :___/___/____	_____:_____AM _____:_____PM	Reflect Affirm Release Connect	
Saturday Date :___/___/____	_____:_____AM _____:_____PM	Reflect Affirm Release Connect	
Sunday Date :___/___/____	_____:_____AM _____:_____PM	Reflect Affirm Release Connect	

Identify one action, feeling or thought you would like to work on this week. Use the section below to outline your area of growth and remember to review it at the end of the week.

Grow

This week I will work on positive: **Feelings   Actions   Thoughts**
What is one thing I can do this week to achieve positive progress?

_____

_____

_____

Dear Diary,

Reflect
What do I see when I look at me?

Affirm
Write 10 positive " I AM" affirmations.

1. I AM _____

2. I AM _____

3. I AM _____

4. I AM _____

5. I AM _____

6. I AM _____

7. I AM _____

8. I AM _____

9. I AM _____

10. I AM _____

What affirmation stands out the most to you?

I AM _____

Affirmations For Moments Of Discouragement

I display a new nature because **I am** a new person, created in God's likeness – holy and true. **Ephesians 4:24**

I am full with the joy of the Lord. **Isaiah 42:10**

I am fearfully and wonderfully made by God." **Psalm 139:14**

I feel most positive when I...

_____
_____
_____
_____
_____
_____
_____
_____
_____
_____
_____
_____
_____
_____
_____
_____
_____
_____
_____
_____
_____
_____
_____
_____
_____
_____
_____
_____
_____

Release

Philippians 4:6-7

Be anxious for nothing, but in everything by prayer and supplication with thanksgiving let your requests be made known to God. And the peace of God, which surpasses all comprehension, will guard your hearts and your minds in Christ Jesus.

What are you struggling with today? What emotions have you battled this week?

_____

_____

_____

_____

_____

_____

_____

_____

_____

_____

_____

_____

_____

_____

_____

_____

_____

_____

_____

_____

_____

_____

Connect

What do I struggle the most with in my life right now?

_____

_____

_____

_____

_____

_____

_____

_____

_____

What can I do today to move beyond the struggle and into the peace
of God?

_____

_____

_____

_____

_____

_____

_____

_____

_____

_____

_____

Dear God help me to choose joy instead of anger. Help me to choose peace instead of power. Help me to trust in your power instead of my plan. Help me to elevate your name instead of my own.
-Anurag Prakash Ray

Dear God,

Lessons Learned

The wound is the place where the Light enters you.
— *Jalaluddin Rumi*

Plan, Focus, Grow

Designate a specific day and time for writing, be realistic but also challenge yourself.
Successful journaling is all about consistently committing to your process. Use the table below to
outline your writing schedule for one week.

Day	Time	Focus *Circle only one per day*
Monday Date :___/___/____	_____:_____AM _____:_____PM	Reflect Affirm Release Connect
Tuesday Date :___/___/____	_____:_____AM _____:_____PM	Reflect Affirm Release Connect
Wednesday Date :___/___/____	_____:_____AM _____:_____PM	Reflect Affirm Release Connect
Thursday Date :___/___/____	_____:_____AM _____:_____PM	Reflect Affirm Release Connect
Friday Date :___/___/____	_____:_____AM _____:_____PM	Reflect Affirm Release Connect
Saturday Date :___/___/____	_____:_____AM _____:_____PM	Reflect Affirm Release Connect
Sunday Date :___/___/____	_____:_____AM _____:_____PM	Reflect Affirm Release Connect

Identify one action, feeling or thought you would like to work on this week. Use the section below to outline your area of growth and remember to review it at the end of the week.

Grow

This week I will work on positive: **Feelings   Actions   Thoughts**

What is one thing I can do this week to achieve positive progress?

_____

_____

_____

Dear Diary,

_____
_____
_____
_____
_____
_____
_____
_____
_____
_____
_____
_____
_____
_____
_____
_____
_____
_____
_____
_____
_____
_____
_____
_____
_____
_____

Release

Exodus 15:26
I am the LORD, who heals you."

Lord, help me to release…
(Be transparent, think of all the things that may have hurt you. Release them to the healer)

_____

_____

_____

_____

_____

_____

_____

_____

_____

_____

_____

_____

_____

_____

_____

_____

_____

_____

_____

_____

_____

_____

_____

I release the pains of my past and trust in you for healing.

Affirm
(Write an encouraging letter to your future self)

Dear future me,

_____

_____

_____

_____

_____

_____

_____

_____

_____

_____

_____

_____

_____

_____

_____

_____

_____

_____

_____

_____

_____

_____

Empty yourself from Grudges, Be honest while praying to God in your conversation with him.- Kishore Bansal

Dear God,

_____

_____

_____

_____

_____

_____

_____

_____

_____

_____

_____

_____

_____

_____

_____

_____

_____

_____

_____

_____

_____

_____

_____

_____

Bigger Than Me

There is no exercise better for the heart than reaching down and lifting people up.

-John Holmes

Plan, Focus, Grow

Designate a specific day and time for writing, be realistic but also challenge yourself. Successful journaling is all about consistently committing to your process. Use the table below to outline your writing schedule for one week.

Day	Time	Focus
		Circle only one per day
Monday Date :___/___/____	_____:_____AM _____:_____PM	Reflect Affirm Release Connect
Tuesday Date :___/___/____	_____:_____AM _____:_____PM	Reflect Affirm Release Connect
Wednesday Date :___/___/____	_____:_____AM _____:_____PM	Reflect Affirm Release Connect
Thursday Date :___/___/____	_____:_____AM _____:_____PM	Reflect Affirm Release Connect
Friday Date :___/___/____	_____:_____AM _____:_____PM	Reflect Affirm Release Connect
Saturday Date :___/___/____	_____:_____AM _____:_____PM	Reflect Affirm Release Connect
Sunday Date :___/___/____	_____:_____AM _____:_____PM	Reflect Affirm Release Connect

Identify one action, feeling or thought you would like to work on this week. Use the section below to outline your area of growth and remember to review it at the end of the week.

Grow

This week I will work on positive: **Feelings Actions Thoughts**

What is one thing I can do this week to achieve positive progress?

_____

_____

_____

Dear Diary,

Check Point

Focus
(Select one focus word)

☐ *Faith*   ☐ *Trust*

☐ *Freedom* ☐ *Patience*

Define your focus:
(briefly describe what your focus word means to you)

_____

_____

_____

_____

3 Ways I will focus on _____ today?

1. _____

2. _____

3. _____

Why is this focus important to me?

_____

_____

_____

_____

_____

Connect Challenge

Reach out to an old friend or relative today. Schedule a lunch or dinner with a college or potential business partner. Do something that makes you uncomfortable in the best way!

Reflect
How can I help someone else ?

I will
(What actions can you take to making a difference in your life and each life you encounter?)

_____

_____

_____

_____

_____

_____

_____

_____

_____

_____

_____

_____

_____

_____

_____

_____

_____

_____

_____

_____

_____

_____

_____

_____

*I **AM** enough to make a difference!*

48

Release

What stops you from believing that you can make a difference?

Dear God,

_____

_____

_____

_____

_____

_____

_____

_____

꙰)꙰

Dear God, please give me strength when I am weak, love when I feel forsaken, courage when I am afraid, wisdom when I am foolish, comfort when I am alone, hope when I feel rejected, and peace when I am in turmoil.
-David Kreger

꙰)꙰

_____

_____

_____

_____

_____

_____

_____

_____

_____

_____

_____

_____

_____

_____

_____

_____

_____

Shift

God, grant me the serenity to accept the things I cannot change, courage to change the things I can, and the wisdom to know the difference.

Reinhold Niebuhr

Plan, Focus, Grow

Designate a specific day and time for writing, be realistic but also challenge yourself. Successful journaling is all about consistently committing to your process. Use the table below to outline your writing schedule for one week.

Day	Time	Focus *Circle only one per day*
Monday Date :___/___/____	_____:_____AM _____:_____PM	Reflect Affirm Release Connect
Tuesday Date :___/___/____	_____:_____AM _____:_____PM	Reflect Affirm Release Connect
Wednesday Date :___/___/____	_____:_____AM _____:_____PM	Reflect Affirm Release Connect
Thursday Date :___/___/____	_____:_____AM _____:_____PM	Reflect Affirm Release Connect
Friday Date :___/___/____	_____:_____AM _____:_____PM	Reflect Affirm Release Connect
Saturday Date :___/___/____	_____:_____AM _____:_____PM	Reflect Affirm Release Connect
Sunday Date :___/___/____	_____:_____AM _____:_____PM	Reflect Affirm Release Connect

Identify one action, feeling or thought you would like to work on this week. Use the section below to outline your area of growth and remember to review it at the end of the week.

Grow

This week I will work on positive: **Feelings   Actions   Thoughts**

What is one thing I can do this week to achieve positive progress?

_____

_____

_____

Dear Diary,

Reflect
What do I need to release to reach my next level?

_____

_____

_____

_____

_____

_____

_____

_____

_____

_____

_____

_____

_____

_____

_____

_____

_____

_____

_____

_____

_____

_____

_____

_____

Affirm

My faith makes me whole in spirit, soul and body.
Mark 5:34

I have faith to overcome...

Release

What can you release as you shift from hurt to healing?

_____

_____

_____

_____

_____

_____

_____

_____

_____

_____

_____

_____

_____

_____

_____

_____

_____

_____

_____

_____

Dear God,

_____

_____

_____

_____

_____

_____

_____

_____

_____

_____

_____

_____

_____

_____

_____

_____

_____

_____

_____

_____

_____

_____

_____

_____

_____

_____

_____

<u>Check Point</u>

<u>*Focus*</u>
(Select one focus word)

☐ *Faith* ☐ *Trust*

☐ *Freedom* ☐ *Patience*

Define your focus:
(briefly describe what your focus word means to you)

_____

_____

_____

_____

3 Ways I will focus on _____ today?

1. _____

2. _____

3. _____

<u>**Why is this focus important to me?**</u>

_____

_____

_____

_____

_____

_____

> ### Be Present
> *Disconnect from television social media and cell phones for 3 hours today. Go out for a walk, read a book or enjoy quiet meditation. Imagine a world with no distractions...*

Reflect
What makes me happy?

_____

_____

_____

_____

_____

_____

_____

_____

_____

_____

_____

_____

_____

_____

_____

_____

_____

_____

_____

_____

_____

_____

Reflection Activity

10 Things that matter the most to me right now.

1. _____

2. _____

3. _____

4. _____

5. _____

6. _____

7. _____

8. _____

9. _____

10. _____

What (on the list) will still matter in one year?

_____
_____
_____
_____
_____
_____
_____

Write a line through the items on the list that will not matter in one year.

Love

Empty pockets never held anyone back. Only empty heads and empty hearts can do that.
- Norman Vincent Peale

Plan, Focus, Grow

Designate a specific day and time for writing, be realistic but also challenge yourself. Successful journaling is all about consistently committing to your process. Use the table below to outline your writing schedule for one week.

Day	Time	Focus *Circle only one per day*
Monday Date :___/___/____	_____:_____AM _____:_____PM	Reflect Affirm Release Connect
Tuesday Date :___/___/____	_____:_____AM _____:_____PM	Reflect Affirm Release Connect
Wednesday Date :___/___/____	_____:_____AM _____:_____PM	Reflect Affirm Release Connect
Thursday Date :___/___/____	_____:_____AM _____:_____PM	Reflect Affirm Release Connect
Friday Date :___/___/____	_____:_____AM _____:_____PM	Reflect Affirm Release Connect
Saturday Date :___/___/____	_____:_____AM _____:_____PM	Reflect Affirm Release Connect
Sunday Date :___/___/____	_____:_____AM _____:_____PM	Reflect Affirm Release Connect

Identify one action, feeling or thought you would like to work on this week. Use the section below to outline your area of growth and remember to review it at the end of the week.

Grow

This week I will work on positive: **Feelings   Actions   Thoughts**

What is one thing I can do this week to achieve positive progress?

_____

_____

_____

Dear Diary,

Reflect
How can I love myself more?

_____

_____

_____

_____

_____

_____

_____

_____

_____

_____

_____

_____

_____

_____

_____

_____

_____

_____

_____

_____

_____

_____

_____

Affirm

1 Corinthians 13:4-7 (NIV)

[4] **Love is** patient, **love is** kind. It does not envy, it does not boast, it is not proud. [5] It does not dishonor others, it is not self-seeking, it is not easily angered, it keeps no record of wrongs. [6] **Love does** not delight in evil but rejoices with the truth. [7] It always protects, always trusts, always hopes, always perseveres.

Love is...

_____
_____
_____
_____
_____
_____
_____
_____
_____
_____
_____
_____
_____
_____
_____
_____
_____
_____
_____
_____
_____
_____
_____
_____

Release

Love is not...

Dear God,

Butterfly

Just when the caterpillar thought the world was over, it became a butterfly.

Plan, Focus, Grow

Designate a specific day and time for writing, be realistic but also challenge yourself.
Successful journaling is all about consistently committing to your process. Use the table below to
outline your writing schedule for one week.

Day	Time	Focus *Circle only one per day*
Monday Date :___/___/____	_____:_____AM _____:_____PM	Reflect Affirm Release Connect
Tuesday Date :___/___/____	_____:_____AM _____:_____PM	Reflect Affirm Release Connect
Wednesday Date :___/___/____	_____:_____AM _____:_____PM	Reflect Affirm Release Connect
Thursday Date :___/___/____	_____:_____AM _____:_____PM	Reflect Affirm Release Connect
Friday Date :___/___/____	_____:_____AM _____:_____PM	Reflect Affirm Release Connect
Saturday Date :___/___/____	_____:_____AM _____:_____PM	Reflect Affirm Release Connect
Sunday Date :___/___/____	_____:_____AM _____:_____PM	Reflect Affirm Release Connect

Identify one action, feeling or thought you would like to work on this week. Use the section below to outline your area of growth and remember to review it at the end of the week.

Grow

This week I will work on positive: **Feelings   Actions   Thoughts**
What is one thing I can do this week to achieve positive progress?

_____

_____

_____

Dear Diary,

Reflect
What does healing feel like to me?

_____
_____
_____
_____
_____
_____
_____
_____
_____
_____
_____
_____
_____
_____
_____
_____
_____
_____
_____
_____
_____
_____
_____

Affirm

I am healed from...

_____

_____

_____

_____

_____

_____

_____

_____

_____

_____

_____

_____

_____

_____

_____

_____

_____

_____

_____

_____

_____

_____

_____

_____

Check Point

Focus
(Select one focus word)

☐ *Faith*   ☐ *Trust*

☐ *Freedom* ☐ *Patience*

Define your focus:
(briefly describe what your focus
word means to you)

_____

_____

_____

_____

3 Ways I will focus on _____ today?

1. _____

2. _____

3. _____

Why is this focus important to me? _____

_____

_____

_____

_____

_____

> Celebrate Progress
> *Reward yourself today with a*
> *special treat.*

Release

I have overcome...

_____
_____
_____
_____
_____
_____
_____
_____
_____
_____
_____
_____
_____
_____
_____
_____
_____
_____
_____
_____
_____
_____
_____

Connect

Dear God,

_____
_____
_____
_____
_____
_____
_____
_____
_____
_____
_____
_____
_____
_____
_____
_____
_____
_____
_____
_____
_____
_____
_____
_____
_____
_____
_____
_____
_____
_____

What lies behind us and what lies before us are tiny matters compared to what lies within us."

-Ralph Waldo Emerson

ABOUT THE CREATOR

Belarria Eichelberger

Belarria Eichelberger is a wife, mother and owner of ByBe's & Friends Mobile Café. She is active in her church and community and enjoys helping others. Belarria is actively completing a vigorous curriculum to become a master cosmetologist in Jacksonville, FL.

www.ingramcontent.com/pod-product-compliance
Lightning Source LLC
Chambersburg PA
CBHW051735040426

42447CB00008B/1143